D1645895

DARTS

Fifty Ways to Play the Game

Jabez Gotobed

THE OLEANDER PRESS

The Oleander Press
16 Orchard Street
Cambridge
CB1 1JT
www.oleanderpress.com

ISBN: 9780900891724

Contents

The Darts Board   5
The Darts Themselves   7
1. The Standard Game   9
2. Bingo   11
3. Killer   12
4. Bowls Darts   13
5. Bulls Only   14
6. Mickey Mouse   15
7. The Knockout   16
8. Getting Better   17
9. Cricket   18
10. Flat Earth   19
11. Halve It!   20
12. The Royal Standard   21
13. Once Round the Island   22
14. Quickly Round the Island   23
15. Snap Darts   24
16. Green Against Red   25
17. Odd Man In   27
18. Noughts and Crosses   28
19. Level Pegging   29
20. Marilyn Monroe   30
21. Checkmate   31
22. The Precipice   32
23. Through the Hoop   33
24. The Colander   35
25. Wimbledon Darts   36
26. Shanghai   37
27. Speedway   38
28. Hound and Hare   39

29. St. Andrews   40
30. Tightrope Walker   42
31. Quoits   43
32. The Relief of Mafeking   44
33. Rounders   45
34. Tyke Towns   46
35. Ibrox   47
36. Robin Hood   49
37. Shove Ha'penny   50
38. Celebration Darts   51
39. Follow-My-Leader With One   52
40. Follow-My-Leader With Three   53
41. Grand National   54
42. General Election   55
43. Pontoon   57
44. Top of the Pops   58
45. Billiards   59
46. Share-Out One-O-One   60
47. White City Dogs   61
48. Triangles   62
49. Scram   63
50. Solo Darts   64
Handicapping   65
Party Games   66
It's Your Turn!   67

The Darts Board

The original board was a keg of ale on its side, marked with three concentric circles. The off-duty archer scored three if his broken arrow landed in the inner circle (hence the modern 'treble'), two if it landed in the middle circle (hence the modern 'double'), and one if it landed in the outer circle.

Later on, more elaborate boards developed. The 'Lincoln' board has no trebles and only one bullseye. The 'Manchester' board has no trebles and both bullseyes. The standard 'London' board, the one used in all national and international tournaments, is however the board for which the games in this book have been devised. The number 20 is black and stands at the top of the board. The distance from the centre of the board vertically to the floor is 1.73 metres, corresponding to 5 feet 8 inches. The board is 45.7 centimetres across (18 inches) and the scoring area from the outermost ring (double to double) is 21 centimetres (8.25 inches). The inner bull is a circle 1.3 centimetres in diameter (0.5 inches) and the outer bull is a circle 3.2 centimetres in diameter (1.25 inches). Normal scoring for an inner bull is 50, and 25 for the outer bull.

In tournament play, an oche or hockey is set up as a marker, behind which players must stand if the throw is to count as valid. The News of the World Championship required players to stand behind an oche set at a minimum throwing distance of 2.44 metres (8 feet) from the board, but the World Darts Federation and the British Darts Organisation have fixed the oche at 2.37 metres (7 feet 9.25 inches). No player must tread on any part of the oche: his feet must be behind the toe edge. A nine foot oche is used locally in parts of London, Birmingham, Manchester, and North-East England. Somewhere or other in England you can find throws of 7.5 feet, 6.5 feet, and 6 feet. So watch the oche when you're travelling: you might be in for a surprise!

The Darts Themselves

Excellent players can make the crudest dart sing, but the average to good player will want to obtain the most accurate available type of dart. At the cheaper end of the scale is the brass dart, with the disadvantage that its fatness makes close bunching difficult. Some players will prefer the slightly more slender nickel silver dart. But the really slim nickel-tungsten dart is a masterpiece of engineering, allowing tight bunching even in the inner bull.

There are so many different types of dart that the novice is bemused, and should ask for advice from an experienced player before choosing darts. He should practise with different weights, barrels, and flights available at a local club, until he finds a dart with which he feels particularly comfortable. Give a dart time to 'settle in'.

How you hold a dart again is a matter of habit and usage. Many players prefer to hold the dart between the thumb (underneath) and the first and second fingers above. Keep an even grip, but not too tight so that you lose sensitivity or eventually suffer from cramp. Keep your stance well poised between leaning too far forward and leaning too far back, but avoid rigidity. For consistency, release the dart at the same moment of each it throw – neither earlier nor later. Avoid jerking the dart out of your hand, or 'chucking it', as beginners do. The movement of the arm must be rhythmic, the release carefully timed, and the follow-through even. Movement should be neither hasty nor languid. The body, shoulders, and elbows should be kept in a similar pose throughout a game, allowing flexibility only to the upper arm and wrist, where the accuracy is determined. Remember to practise whenever you can, without reaching boredom. And never allow your mind to be preoccupied with success or failure, but simply treat the next dart as if it were your first and last. Enjoy your darts, vary your practice, and increase your enjoyment of the game by taking advantage of some of the traditional games (such as Shanghai and Shove Ha'penny) and the many new games recommended here for your pleasure.

1. The Standard Game

Number of players: Two, or two teams consisting of 8 or 9 players each
Number of darts: Three each

Most darts leagues have their rules set out in their own rules-books and fixture lists. Such rules are not uniform, differences being hallowed by local usage over a long period of time, but most of the following suggestions will be acceptable to most secretaries.

Each game goes to the player or team who first scores the exact number 501, both starting and finishing on a double. A full game consists of the best of three 'legs'. (Inner bulls, otherwise counting 50, do not count as doubles in many League matches, so settle this point at the outset).

Two points are awarded to the player or team who wins the most games, except that if eight singles are shared equally between two teams, then so are the two points.

Score cards signed by both captains are posted the morning after the game to the League secretary. If a team does not make an appearance at the agreed time and place, it forfeits both points. If either team is short of the agreed number of players at the beginning of a game, an equal number of players is nominated by the team captains and the full team receives the balance of points as forfeit. Adequate notice of postponement – normally 72 hours – must be submitted by first-class post to the League secretary and to the opposing team, otherwise the match is forfeited by the postponing team.

Any club fielding an ineligible player, not registered with the League secretary, forfeits both points. The home team provides the scorer. The visiting team plays first and provides the score-checker. Club secretaries are obliged to exchange team-lists not later than 48 hours before the match is due: failure to do so involves a club fine to be imposed by the League. No gambling is permitted on official league or cup matches.

Variations on scoring in the Standard Game include 301, 701, 1001 and even higher in the marathon fixtures arranged between famous champions.

2. Bingo

Number of players: Any number, the more the merrier
Number of darts: One each

A Master of Ceremonies selected by lot calls any number from one to twenty, drawn blind from 20 numbered small pieces in a hat. Each player must now throw that number, scoring 1 for a single, 2 for a double or outer bull, or 3 for a treble or inner bull. Each player puts 50 pence in the kitty.

     The first player to score 17 points over a minimum of six rounds has a 'full house' and calls 'bingo' to scoop the kitty.

3. Killer

Number of players: Two or more
Number of darts: Three each

Several games have this name, but the most familiar is confined to doubles. The player who wins the toss nominates a double, and keeps throwing until he hits it or until he has thrown all three darts, whichever is earlier. Player 2 nominates a different double, and tries to do the same as Player 1. Each player, after hitting his own double, is then released to throw at his opponent's double. Each has three 'lives' (or five in a variant) and loses one 'life' every time an opponent hits his double.

The winner is the player left with one or more lives when all the other players are defeated.

Another game called 'Killer' is really a variant of 'Getting Better', but uses the same principle of three or five 'lives' as the game above.

4. Bowls Darts

Number of players: Two
Number of darts: Three each

As in bowls, the object is to finish nearer a target than your opponent, but in this case the 'jack' to aim for is the inner bull, which counts two, or the outer bull, which counts one, both scores being additional to any points scored for proximity.

Player 1, having won the toss, throws three darts as near the inner bull as possible. The scores on the outer face of the board are ignored. Player 2 now tries to throw his three darts nearer the centre than those of Player 1. If Player 2 succeeds with one dart, but his other two are farther from the centre than those of Player 1, he scores 1. He scores an additional 1 if the scoring dart lies in the outer bull, or an additional 2 if in the inner bull. In the event of both players having their nearest dart equidistant to the centre, a 1-1 draw is proclaimed. As in bowls, a player with all three nearer than his opponent's three will score a 3-0 win. The object is to score more points than your opponent over 9 or 18 'holes', and if you finish level, you go to the '10th' or the '19th' for the decider.

5. Bulls Only

Number of players: Any number
Number of darts: Three each

In this game, the outside numbers are ignored, and the game is settled by accurate bull-shooting. The player who wins the toss throws first, and scores 3 points for every outer bull, and five points for every inner bull. Any dart failing to land within the outer numbers is withdrawn from the following round only. The winner is the player who teaches eleven points first (or twenty-two, for a longer game), so that at least three bulls must be scored (or four if they are all outer bulls) to win.

This can be especially exciting in the later stages, when four or five players might be on 9 or 10.

6. Mickey Mouse

Number of players: Two or four
Number of darts: Three each

The numbers from 20 to 11 are written vertically on the board, with 20 at the top and Bull at the bottom, below 11.

Player A throws first, having won the toss, to score 3 of any number he chooses (including the bull, understood as both inner and outer), a 3 counting as a treble, a double and a single, or three singles. Then Player B throws three darts. Once 3 of a number are scored, that player may start scoring the numerical value of that number until his opponent (or the opposing team in doubles) has scored three of the same number and 'kills' or neutralises the scores.

As one might 'declare' in cricket, so a player or team with a high score might decide to stop scoring plus points and concentrate instead on wiping out the opposing scoring possibilities.

The game is over when every number has been hit three times: the winner is the team with the higher points total. It is a tactical game, and is called 'Tactics' in some parts of the country.

7. The Knockout

Number of players: Everybody
Number of darts: Three each

The names of all participants in the room are written on torn-up slips of paper, then drawn in the manner of any cup draw. Byes are drawn in such a way as to produce a final pairing of sixteen or eight players.

The player first out of the draw then tries to score as many points as possible by the usual scoring system. The second player out of the draw then tries to beat that total and, if successful, goes through to the next round to meet the winner of the next pairing. In the event of a draw, a fourth (and if necessary, a fifth) dart is thrown by each player to produce an outright winner in each brief match.

The Knockout can be played once a week or once a month on a regular day: it has the advantage of bringing everyone in, and the excitement of any 'sudden death' game.

8. Getting Better

Number of players: Any number, for a musical chairs-style knockout tournament
Number of darts: One each

Each participant writes his name in a list on the scoreboard and when no more come forward a line is drawn under the last name. Each player then throws one dart in the order shown on the scoreboard except that if the dart scores lower (or the same) as the previous dart, he is out, and his name is crossed through. A typical Getting Better result would look something like this:

A-14; B-double 8 = 16; C-11 (so out); D-20; E-20 (so out); F-25; A-double 20 : 40; B-treble 7 (so out); D-treble 16 — 48; F-3 (so out); A—2O (so out). Therefore D is the winner.

9. Cricket

Number of players: Two teams of eleven players each, preferably from two different villages who are cricket rivals
Number of darts: Six (as in a cricket over)

The team first 'in' to 'bat' will select two players. The 'opening bat' will try to score a 6, or a 4, and 1, 2, and 3 are also permissible, though doubles and trebles are not (except treble 1 and 2, or double 1, 2 and 3). An outer bull scores 4, and an inner bull 6. If the 'batsman' scores an odd number of 'runs', then his partner takes over, as in cricket. A player is 'out' when he fails to score a permitted 'run' and the next player is in. An innings is over when ten 'batsmen' are out, and the opposing team is set the task of beating that total. A player is 'caught' if a dart lands outside the doubles circle.

There are many variations of this game, including the five-a-side or six-a-side.

10. Flat Earth

Number of players: Two
Number of darts: Three each

There is no difference between this game and any other game of darts, except that the board is adjusted three times after the first game. Once so that '20' is pointing east, then again so it is pointing south, and finally so it is pointing west. It is peculiar how even the best players seem to be shattered out of their routine by these simple changes. Some are never the same again. The game was given its title after a player said it proved that the earth was flat.

This game cannot be played with boards fixed to a wall, but many are only hooked on. Playing with a board propped up on a table or ledge at a different height from normal can be good practice for eye-and-wrist co-ordination. Just try it once.

One flat earth game is to place the board flat on the floor, and throw not across but downwards. This is a much safer outdoors game, on grass, than the conventional game with the hanging board, but it takes some practice to get accustomed to the 45-degree angle of the dart's entry into the board. You needn't play with a board, of course: the darts can be thrown at a rubber quoit on the grass, or on matting.

11. Halve It!

Number of players: Any number
Number of darts: Three each

The left-hand column of the scoreboard is marked with between a dozen and twenty numbers, such as – in descending order – 9, any double, 10, 11, outer ring, 12, 13, inner ring, 14, 15, any treble, 16, 17, outer or inner bull, 18, 19, 20.

The initials of each player are then set across the top of the scoreboard in reverse alphabetical order.

Player A now aims for the single 9, and scores as many nines as possible to a maximum of 3 = 27. Player B now aims for the same, and so on until everyone has played. Anyone missing the target with all three darts in three successive rounds is eliminated.

The snag is that, if you miss with all three darts in any one round, your total previous scored is halved, so that consistency is all in this game, and it is quite possible for a player to lead in every round except the last, and then lose. The dreaded cry of "Halve It!" penalises brilliant but erratic players in favour of the solid and careful.

12. The Royal Standard

Number of players: Two
Number of darts: Two each

There are many variations of this game, but the standard formula quoted here comes from a pub in Hayes (Middlesex) called 'The Royal Standard'.

Player 1 tries to score as high as possible with only two darts, and Player 2 tries to score higher, over ten rounds (or fifteen), each round being scored separately. The scoring is simplified in that only the winner scores: 1 point if his total is 1-10 points higher than his rival's; 2 points for a lead of 11-20; 3 points for a lead of 21-30; and so on. However, points for poor play are deducted, so that a player loses 1 of his points at the end for each round in which his total was 29 or less. Typical results over 15 rounds are 11-10 and 15-17.

The Royal Standard game works well in tournament play.

13. Once Round the Island

Number of players: Two
Number of darts: Three each

Possibly one of the most popular of darts games, 'Once Round the Island' is a true test of skill. The player who wins the toss tries to throw a 1 (or 1 double or 1 treble or either bull). If he throws it, he tries 2, and then 3, and so on, alternating every three darts with his opponent who is chasing the same target. The winner is the player who first lands each number from 1 to 20. If you fail to score a number, you must keep trying to get that number until you succeed, so it is theoretically possible to overtake a player from 13-19 to 20-19 and I have seen it done. In my experience the number '6' causes the most hiccups: what is your experience?

This game is also called 'Round the Board' and 'Round the Clock'.

In a variant called 'Doubles Round the Island', two partners (playing 1A, 2A, IB, 2B) carry on from each other's score to try to defeat the opposition. The game lasts just as long as the original game, but involves twice as many players.

14. Quickly Round the Island

Number of players: Two
Number of darts: Three each

This variant of 'Once Round the Island' is played to a limited number of rounds of three darts each (usually ten or twelve) or to a limited time (usually five to seven minutes). The winner is the player who has progressed farther towards 20 at the end of the limited period.

In the variant called 'All Hands Round the Island', skill is at an even higher premium than in the original, for a player who scores a double misses out the next target, and a player who scores a treble misses out the next two targets, so a great player could win in three rounds like this: treble 1, treble 4, double 7; treble 9, 12, treble 13; treble 16, 19, 20. This is an actual score recorded in Glasgow in 1979.

15. Snap Darts

Number of players: Two at a time
Number of darts: Three each

Snap requires two identical darts boards placed side by side with two identical oches, and two players of roughly comparable skill.

A game consists of ten rounds of three darts each, and by mutual agreement can follow the numbers 1 to 10 inclusive around the board, or the numbers 11 to 20. The object is for each player to throw on the calls 'One, two, three' while throwing each dart. 'Snap' is called immediately after throwing if both players throw a single, both a double, or both a treble on the nominated number. If they both throw wrongly – that is, on a number not nominated, they may not call 'Snap'. Each player gets 1 for the right single, 2 for the right double, and 3 for the right treble, plus the opponent's 1, 2 or 3 (as applicable) if he has called 'Snap' before his opponent. An umpire is vital in this game to prevent argument, and any player questioning the umpire's decision shall irrevocably forfeit that point. If 'Snap' is called wrongly, the player so calling shall lose 4 points. The umpire shall warn a player not throwing on the spoken cue to throw, and has the power to disqualify a player's score in any round when that player repeatedly throws late.

16. Green Against Red

Number of players: Two or four
Number of darts: Three each

The player who wins the toss elects to throw for the green doubles and trebles on the standard board, totalling 540 points, including the outer bull. The opposing player or team then has to throw for the red doubles and trebles on the board, totalling 535 points, excluding the inner bull. Player 1 aims at the double 1 or treble 1, and scores 5 for every treble and three for every double except that only 1 double and 1 treble maximum may be scored out of three darts. A dart landing in a single 1 counts nothing, but if it lands in any other single it counts one away, in a wrong double two away, and in a wrong treble three away.

Player 2 then aims in the same way for double and treble 20 (but only one of each) and so on in an anticlockwise direction until each has had ten rounds.

Another method, simpler to score, involves the use of the actual double and treble totals around the board, again counting green doubles and trebles for the Green player, and red doubles and trebles for the Red player. Champions will want to use the rule penalizing a player throwing on to his opponent's colour by deducting a single, double, or treble of the wrong number thrown. So a first round might score like this:

Green: Treble 1 = 3, double 5 (nothing), 1. Total 4. Red: Double 20 = 40, treble 5 = -15 (wrong colour), Treble 20 = 60. Total 85.

If the scoring seems unequal, it must be remembered that it evens out over the 10 rounds, when the aggregate scores determine the winner.

17. Odd Man In

Number of players: Any number
Number of darts: Two each

A musical-chairs type of game for participants at all levels. The idea is to score any odd number over 10, including the outer bull (but not, of course, the inner bull), with each dart of two. A player drops out as soon as a dart fails to score 11, 13, 15, etc. up to 57 (treble 19). This 'sudden-death' type of game attracts many people who would not ordinarily play darts. The last 'odd man in' is the winner.

18. Noughts and Crosses

Number of players: Two or four
Number of darts: Three each

Draw a noughts and crosses shape of nine spaces, three by three, on the scoreboard. Then write 50 in the centre, and eight different scores (all thirteens, treble 8, double 2, etc.) in the other spaces. The aim is for one player or team to complete a straight line of three. Every time a target is achieved (one player or team scoring three thirteens out of three achieves 'all thirteens'), then the initials of the player or team captain replace the figures on the board. As in noughts and crosses, the losing players must often aim to frustrate a line of three being notched by the opposition, rather than concentrating on attacking a positive line of their own.

To make the game easier, single numbers can fill eight, or even all nine, spaces.

19. Level Pegging

Number of players: Two, and an umpire
Number of darts: Three each, and one for the umpire

The umpire throws his dart to begin play, normally not at 20 (which suffers the most wear on the average board). The aim of both players in each of ten rounds is to score exactly the same with each dart as the umpire scored with his, and the two players score one point. Only for those darts which are 'level pegging' with the umpire's. So a typical round might end 2-1 for Player 1 if the umpire throws a 19. Player 1: treble 19 (counts nothing), 19, 19; Player 2: 17, 19, double 19 (counts nothing). The winner is the player who has scored the most points after ten rounds, although in one variant a point is deducted every time a player throws outside the doubles circle.

20. Marilyn Monroe

Number of players: Any number
Number of darts: Six each

This is one of the many games which use an alphabetical equivalent for the numbers on the board. The generally-accepted equivalents in the Rhondda Valley are:

A-1, B-2, C-3, D-4, E-5, F-6, G-7, H and 1-8, J and K-9, L-10, M-11, N-12, O-13, P and Q-14, R-15, S-16, T-17, U and V-18, W-19, X, Y and Z-20.

Starting with Marilyn Monroe, and using the names of as many film stars as you like, the players then take it in turns to see how few darts they need to spell out the name. So, Marilyn Monroe needs the following score in succession: 11, 1, 15, 8, 10, 20, 12, 11, 13, 12, 15, 13, 5. A very good player might take only fifteen darts to spell out the 13 letters. To avoid argument, it is good practice to spell the name on the scoreboard before you start, not afterwards.

Doubles and trebles count as singles here, as a rule.

21. Checkmate

Number of players: Two
Number of darts: Five each

Singles on the board count as pawns, doubles as knights, trebles as bishops, the outer bull as the Queen, and the inner bull as the King.

Player 1, having won the toss, selects 'White' or 'Black', and may throw only on 'his' own colour, except that both players have equal rights to the bullseyes. He throws his five darts as follows:

Pawn, Knight, Pawn, Bishop, Pawn, Queen, Pawn, King.

At the point where he fails to throw this exact sequence, Player 2 begins to throw the same sequence on his own colour, anywhere on the board. 'Checkmate' is called when a player finally throws a King, having previously obtained the rest of the sequence in the correct order, over no matter how many rounds.

The humorous side of the game, when a player throws an inner bull, while wanting any single, corresponds to the 'Too hot!' cry at a tournament when a double 1 is required to finish and the player throws a bull to bust.

22. The Precipice

Number of players: Any number
Number of darts: Three each

Starting at 3, and throwing clockwise, the players aim to throw one dart in each double, until they are back at 3. Having achieved the double, one continues immediately to the next, and the first to finish wins.

'Staying on the Precipice' is identical to 'The Precipice', except that in each round of the 21, beginning and ending at 3, each player tries to score all three darts in the same double, making a possible maximum of 63 points.

'Falling off the Precipice' uses the same rules as the previous game, except that any darts that miss the double and land inside them may be used again in the following round, but darts that miss the double but land outside the doubles circle are not eligible to be thrown in the following round, and then become eligible again in the next.

23. Through the Hoop

Number of players: Two teams of two
Number of darts: Three each

Croquet addicts can play this one during the long winter evenings when the lawn is covered with snow.

Team 1, having won the toss, requires the first player in Team 2 to 'throw a hoop'. That is, the opening player must throw a second or third dart two segments away from his first, though the first can land anywhere except on a bull. If the player opens correctly, play begins. If not, he forfeits nine points and the opening player of Team 1 'throws a hoop'.

When a hoop is thrown, so that for example one dart is on 17 and another on 19 (the third need not be used if two darts suffice), the first player on the opposite side scores for each dart thrown in the segment between the hoop (in this case on the number 3). One is scored for a single, four for a double, and seven for a treble. That round continues with each of the other two players throwing to score. The total of the nine darts is added up towards the final score. The match consists of eight legs, so that each player has the chance to throw a hoop twice, and the winning partnership is the one with the higher points total after the eighth leg. Here is a typical score over two legs:

First leg: Player 1A: 2, 6 (not a hoop), 10 (hoop with 2). Player 2A: 17 (no score), 2 (no score), double 15 (4 points). Total: 4 points.

Player 1B: 15 (1 point), treble 15 (7 points), 10 (no score). Team total: 8 points. Player 2B: double 10 (no score), outer bull (no score), 15 (1 point). Team total: 5 points.

Second leg: Player 2A: 14, 11 (not a hoop), 9 (not a hoop). Total: 9 points away. Player 1A: 20, treble 18 (hoop with 20). Third dart not required. Player 2B: Treble 1 (7 points), 20 (no score), double 1 (4 points). Team total: 2 points. Player 1B: 1 (1 point), double 1 (four points), double 20 (no points). Team total: 5 points.

24. The Colander

Number of players: Any number up to six a side
Number of darts: Two each

You need squares of paper about 6 cm x 6 cm for this game, using one in each round.

The team which wins the toss throws a dart, anywhere on the board, with a square of paper attached in such a way that other darts can also penetrate the paper. The idea is for the other players on the 'home' team to get more darts than their opponents do through the same piece of paper. At the end of the round, expert players will make the piece of paper look like a colander, hence the name of the game.

The second round opens with the 'away' team throwing the 'paper' – dart anywhere on the board. The winning team is the one which has amassed more 'colander' points over 5 or 7 rounds.

If any part of the paper falls outside the doubles circle, the opening throw is generally retaken.

25. Wimbledon Darts

Number of players: Two
Number of darts: Two each (except, when receiving, a player uses only one)

The player who wins the toss 'serves' on a number he has nominated. If he scores a double or treble on the nominated number, he wins the point on an 'ace'. If he serves on the nominated number as a single, the 'ball' is in play and his opponent 'returns' on the same number, winning the point if scoring a treble or double, and keeping the 'ball' in play if scoring a single.

If the 'server' misses the nominated number, 'fault' is called, and he 'serves' again. If the second 'serve' is missed, then 'double fault' is called, and he loses the point. Similarly, once the ball is in play, the player who first misses the nominated number loses the point.

The server then continues to play, scoring as in lawn tennis. A bull for either player is a winning stroke. No number may be nominated more than once in a game, except in the unusual case of a deuce game continuing long enough to use all the numbers on the board.

In the second game, Player 2 serves. Matches consist of three sets or five.

26. Shanghai

Number of players: Two or more
Number of darts: Three each

The player who wins the toss starts by throwing his darts at number 1: single, double, and treble (though not necessarily in that order), and is followed by his opponent or opponents on the same number, then both on number 2, number three, and so on, until one player scores a Shanghai: one single, one double, and one treble.

If two or more players score a Shanghai on the same number, they continue until an outright winner is found. In a variant, the winning of the toss can be advantageous to the player who wins it, because Shanghai is proclaimed without giving the following player a chance to carry on.

Some Shanghai games go up to 7, some to 9, and others farther.

A quicker variant is to nominate some numbers, most frequently 5, 7, and 9; any player not scoring one of these is eliminated.

27. Speedway

Number of players: Two teams of two or four each
Number of darts: Two each

The two teams are Black and White, corresponding to the colours on the traditional 'London' darts board, with number 20 black and number 19 white. The team winning the toss selects Black (which has an aggregate of 107 points), leaving White to the opponents (an aggregate of 103).

There are 13 heats, as in Speedway, and each team may play its best players as 'heat leaders' as in speedway. Bulls are not counted. Each team may score only on its own colour, so that a White player throwing twice on 20 'does not finish' that heat, and scores nothing. The aim is, with a single dart, to make the highest possible score on your own colour. An example might be:

White 1: 19 and double 19 = 57; Black 1:18 and 12 = 30; White 2:7 and 3 = no score (black numbers); Black 2:Bull (no score) and treble 20: 60. The points (here totalling 4 for Black and 2 for White) are calculated as in speedway. A typical score might be 40-37 (one point having been dropped when two players failed to score in one heat).

This game can be played on a home-and-away basis between teams of speedway enthusiasts from different towns.

28. Hound and Hare

Number of players: Two or more
Number of darts: Three each

The player who wins the toss is the Hare, and his opponent or opponents the Hound or Hounds in pursuit.

The Hare travels round the board in a clockwise direction, starting from 20, and moving by one number at a time tries to get back to 20 (or double 20) before the Hounds can catch him. Sometimes the Hounds start from 12 (two behind), sometimes from 5 (one behind), and sometimes from 20. The Hound who first overtakes the Hare is the winner, but a good Hare can win by returning to 20 before the Hounds.

A variant consists of requiring the Hare to score a single and double, while the Hounds need score only a double. In some parts of Britain, this game is known as 'Fox and Hound'.

29. St. Andrews

Number of players: Two or four
Number of darts: Three each

A game adapted from golf can borrow the number of yards at your local golf course as the basis for scoring.

The following is an imaginary course which will serve just as well.

Hole 1-300m, 2-520m, 3-210m, 4-370m, 5-420m, 6-470m, 7-390m, 8-220m, 9-330m.

Hole 10-410m, 11-560m, 12-240m, 13-380, 14-410m, 15-480m, 16-400m, 17-390m, 18-350m.

Omitting the final nought, the aim is to achieve the exact score above in the lowest number of 'strokes', remembering that if one 'overshoots' the 'hole' one can always go back. Thus, Player 1 might throw double 14 = 28, then 7 to total 35, which is beyond the hole, and 'sink the final putt' with a 5. Player 2 might throw a double 10 = 20 and then a 10 to sink in 2 and so go 1 hole up, or score two strokes against three, depending on whether match-play or medal-play is to be adopted at the outset.

A variation is to eliminate doubles and trebles, so that the 390 at hole 17 could only be scored with a 19 and a 20, instead of with a possible treble 13. As always, the 'golfer' with the lower aggregate score wins. The foursome style of play is equally enjoyable.

A handicap system could well be introduced if the game becomes popular enough.

30. Tightrope Walker

Number of players: Two or more
Number of darts: Player 1 has 2; all others have 3 each

The player who wins the toss throws one dart to the married man's side of the central 20 and 3, and the other to the bachelor's. Either dart falling into the bulls or 20 or 3 must be thrown again.

The other players must now throw their darts exactly on the imaginary 'tightrope' between these two darts, in such a way that a ruler (or this book) placed along the two original darts also touches the later dart. Any player 'walking the tightrope' scores a point (or a pint). Each player in turn throws the two points to establish the position of the tightrope, giving all the rest an opportunity to 'walk the tightrope' successfully, and the winner is the player who most often does so.

In a variant, a thread is actually tied from one 'pillar' dart to the other, but this is a bit fussy for most darts enthusiasts: a rough-and-ready ruler, pencil, or book will satisfy most contestants.

31. Quoits

Number of players: Two
Number of darts: Three for Player 2 and one for Player 1

Player 1 throws a dart anywhere on the board, and places a rubber quoit roughly 7 centimetres in diameter over the dart.

Player 2 now has to land his darts inside the quoit and scores 1 point for every single, 2 for every double, 3 for every treble, 4 for every outer bull, and five for every inner bull. Player 1 will therefore avoid throwing his original dart near the centre or in the upper half. If he throws it outside the doubles circle (i.e. off the scoring area) altogether, he concedes six points.

The positions are reversed after round one. The winner is the first to reach 31 points.

32. The Relief of Mafeking

Number of players: Two
Number of darts: Five each

The player who wins the toss sets out to maintain the siege of Mafeking, and to keep within the twenty prisoners who are confined in the bullseyes. For every inner bull he scores, two more prisoners are taken, and for every outer bull, one more. A running total should be chalked up on the scoreboard.

Player 2 can relieve Mafeking (and must do it within 10 rounds or fail in the attempt) by scoring a total of 20 points (or as many more as he needs to, to keep pace with Player 1's progress). Each time Player 2 scores an outer bull he releases four prisoners, and each inner bull releases five prisoners. The progress might begin:

Start: 20 prisoners.

Player 1: -, 2, -, 1, -. Total now: 23 prisoners.

Player 2: -, -, 4, -, 5. Total at the end of round 1: 14 prisoners.

33. Rounders

Number of players: Two teams of four each
Number of darts: Three each

The captain of the team winning the toss goes in to bat, and is set to score 20, 11 (first base), 3 (second base), 6 (third base), and again 20 (home run). Though he has only three darts, and proceeds only one base at a time on scoring a single, he can go one base extra for each double, and two bases extra for each treble. It is therefore possible for a player scoring double 20 to go straight to second base, and double 3 to score a home run.

The team losing the toss spend their three darts each aiming at the inner and outer bull, trying to get the hitter out with an outer bull, and the whole team out with an inner bull. The innings continues until the batting team is out separately or collectively. Then their opponents go into bat. The two captains decide on the number of innings to be played before the match.

34. Tyke Towns

Number of players: Three
Number of darts: Three each

Three commercial travellers are fighting for territory in Yorkshire. The fairest way out is to play darts for it. Each town is represented by a particular combination of three numbers (singles, doubles and trebles all count as singles), except that an inner or outer bull is a 'joker' which can stand for any number the thrower desires. Once a player has thrown the right combination in one set of 3 throws, he 'wins the town' and it is put down to him on the scoreboard. The player to 'win' most towns is the victor. Of course, this Yorkshire game can be adapted to any other county or country.

Halifax 2, 13, 18 Dewsbury 1, 6, 16 Bradford 1, 8, 19 Otley 7, 11, 18 Skipton 4, 12, 14 Leeds 2, 10, 17 Pudsey 3, 10, 15 Ilkley 4, 9, 17 Rotherham 5, 15, 20 Wakefield 7, 12, 20.

35. Ibrox

Number of players: Two
Number of darts: Three each

This is a time-limit game, normally of ten minutes each way, named after Glasgow Rangers' soccer ground. A referee should act as time-keeper, scorer, and arbitrator in the event of dispute.

Team 1 (Black) takes the black segments on the board, and Team 2 (White) just the white segments. The bulls are common to both teams, and a bull counts as a goal to the last player if he was on the attack. The field of play looks like this:

Black Goalkeeper – 20

Black Back Four – 14, 12, 18, 13
White Attack – 5, 1 and Bulls

Black Midfield – 8, 10, 2
White Midfield – 9, 6, 4

Black Attack – 3, 7 and Bulls
White Back Four – 11, 16, 17, 15

White Goalkeeper – 19

The team which wins the toss starts in midfield. If Black win the toss, the player representing Black must throw a 9, 6, or 4 to 'pass the ball' to 3, 7, or a bull. If he does, he must then score a 3, 7, or bull to score a goal. If he fails, the 'ball' may be picked up by the White players, who must score 8, 10 or 2 to intercept. If they do, they must pass to 5, 1 or bull before being able to 'shoot' with one of those numbers. If White fail to intercept, Black have another chance to pass from 9, 6 or 4 to 3, 7 or bull. Whenever a move breaks down, the opposition must try to take over exactly at the point where it breaks down, not in front or behind. Teams may have a two-minute interval between ten-minute halves. The winning side is the one which scores the more goals in the 20-minute game.

Good players will confine scoring play to doubles and trebles.

36. Robin Hood

Number of players: Any number
Number of darts: Three each

Champions can be challenged to transfix a dart
to a length of string, cord, rope or ribbon hung
over the horizontal bar of the '2' on the 20. It
can hang down in single or double strands, and
should reach just below the outer bull, to rank
as the greatest shot ever if the marksman nails
the string to the inner bull!

A game frequently played without a
winner – and there is no consolation prize for
those nearest the string.

37. Shove Ha'penny

Number of players: Two or more
Number of darts: Three each

The player or team winning the toss opens by trying to score three points on the number 1: a single counts 1, a double 2, and a treble 3. A score of more than 3 is lost to the rival team, so that a double followed by another double would score 3 for the playing team and 1 for the opponents. All three darts need not be used, for example in the round when a treble is scored with the first dart. But a winning shot must be earned by the team, not awarded to it by default.

The game is usually confined to the numbers 1 to 9. The winning team is the one with most points at the end of the agreed number of rounds.

38. Celebration Darts

Number of players: Three
Number of darts: Two each

A party or celebration game after a famous victory, or for a birthday or reunion. You need the very small envelopes that florists use for cards sent with bouquets. Or, at a pinch, bigger envelopes could be cut down.

A fiver – or a tenner! – is concealed in one of the three envelopes, and a piece of blank paper the same size as a note in each of the other two. One envelope is pinned just above the 20, one just to the left of the 11, and a third to the right of the 6, so that the bulk of the envelope is on the scoring numbers, but the drawing pins are outside the numbers.

Each of the three players throws a dart at each of two envelopes. If all three or none happen to hit the envelope which, when opened, is found to contain the cash, then the organiser does it all again. If two hit the right envelope, the third drops out, and the organiser does it all again. If one player hits the right envelope, and the other two miss, then the successful player keeps the money.

The better the players, the smaller the envelopes need to be.

39. Follow-My-Leader With One

Number of players: Any number
Number of darts: One for the first to play in each round; three each for the other player or players in that round

The player who wins the toss throws a dart in as difficult a place to follow as possible: either a treble or a bull.

The second player, with three 'lives', now attempts to throw the same score. If he scores on the first attempt he keeps all three 'lives' and the third player throws to make the same score. If he makes the score on the third dart, for example, he loses two 'lives', and if he fails with the third dart he loses all 'lives' and is out of the game.

The winner is the last player to stay in the game with a 'life' left.

40. Follow-My-Leader With Three

Number of players: Any number
Number of darts: Three each

The player who wins the toss throws all three darts. Player 2 now tries to obtain the same total, with any combination of numbers, using three darts – or fewer if needed. He scores 6 points if he obtains Player 1's total with only 1 dart; 4 points if he obtains Player 1's total with only 2 darts; and 2 points if he obtains Player 1's total with three darts.

Player 3 and all the rest now attempt the same. The winner is the player who has amassed most points when each player has thrown three initial darts once, or – if there are very few players – twice or three times as agreed before the match.

A variation is that the first player to score 21 points wins the game.

41. Grand National

Number of players: Any number — the more the merrier
Number of darts: Three each

Each player takes the name of a favourite steeplechase horse, if necessary from the morning paper. Betting on the 'horses' whose 'names are shown on the scoreboard against the names of the players concerned will of course depend on the quality of the players.

Professionals, the 'thoroughbreds', will want to aim for only doubles and trebles.

Nineteen obstacles on the Aintree course are represented by 19 rounds of 3 darts each. In each round the aim is to score 2 or 3 out of the 3 darts in a nominated number, beginning at 20 and going round the course anti-clockwise. Every time a jockey throws one or no dart in the segment required, his horse 'falls' and 'is withdrawn from the race. Every time he throws 2 in the correct number a 'falter' is recorded against his horse on the scoreboard but proceeds to the next number or 'fence'. The winner is the horse which finishes at number 1 with the fewest 'falters', and scoops the kitty. If no player gets to number 1 'round the clock', the kitty is shared in the ratio 3:2:1 between the last to fall, the last but one, and the last but two.

42. General Election

Number of players: Four or five candidates, standing as Labour, Conservative, Communist, LibDem, and perhaps an Independent
Number of darts: Three each

The candidates throw one dart each, highest score starting, second highest second, and so on.

The constituency has a total of 51,000 active voters. A candidate can win 1,000 votes for every consecutive double as he starts anti-clockwise around the board from 9. He keeps on canvassing and winning votes as long as he does not fail.

When he fails, the second candidate begins at 9, and only stops when he fails, and so on.

After all candidates have failed once, the first begins again at the double where he failed last time. The declaration is made when an invincible majority is obtained so that if the poll reads:

F. Seymour, Labour 4,000
J. Rudge, Conservative 7,000
T. Martin, Communist 3,000
E. Dewick, LibDem 8,000
R. Janner, Independent 5,000

then Seymour would need only 14 doubles on his next round to give a total of 18,000 votes with only 9,000 votes to be counted, so Dewick could not capture the seat for the Liberals even if he were to win all remaining votes (which would give him a total of only 17,000).

This is an excellent game to play while waiting for local or national election results.

One variation gives outright victory to any candidate who at any time gains a 9,000 majority over his nearest rival.

43. Pontoon

Number of players: Four
Number of darts: Three each

The object of the game is for three players to achieve the score of 21 against a 'dealer' or 'banker'. Each is banker in turn, in alphabetical order of first name of the players.

The banker, in the first round, throws a dart to score higher than 21: a bull, a double on 11 or higher, or a treble on 8 or higher. If he happens to score a treble 7, he loses five points outright to each of the other three players. If he scores higher than 21, the banker wins the round, and the second player becomes banker. If the banker scores lower than 21, the aim of each player in turn, scoring independently, is to make the total 21, and he scores three points if he makes the number 21 with the first dart, two if he needs two darts, one if he needs three, and none if he fails to reach 21 or 'busts' with a total higher than 21.

The first player to total 21 or more points wins the match.

One variation is for a bull to score 3 for the banker and 2 each for the players. This can be an important ploy if the banker has 18 or 19 or 20 points, and any of the players has the same total for otherwise the banker cannot score when it is his turn as banker.

44. Top of the Pops

Number of players: Any number from 4 to 10
Number of darts: Three each

One for the younger generation. Each player can represent a singer or a pop group, and try to get into the 'top ten' chart. Draw for order of play.

All players start at number 10, aiming for it with all three darts, and scoring 3 for each treble, 2 for each double, and one for each single. The player with the highest total on number 10 goes on to the scoreboard as no. 10: two or more names can go on the board if there is a tie.

Everyone then starts again at number 9, and so on, up to no. 1. When all the 10 rounds are over, the winning singer or group is the one with the most points, scoring 10 points for the no. 1, 9 for the no. 2, 8 for no. 3, 7 for no. 4, 6 for no. 5, 5 for no. 6. 4 for no. 7, 3 for no. 8, 2 for no. 9, and 1 for no. 10. If two players tie for fourth place, they notch up 35 points each, and so on.

Like many darts games. this can rise to a great climax, since the players filling no. 1 and 2 positions have a much better chance of winning at the end than those (if they are different) who won the early rounds for the lower positions.

45. Billiards

Number of players: Two
Number of darts: Three each

The scores in billiards are 2 and 3, and the player with the cue keeps on with a break until he misses.

Billiards darts uses the same principle over 7 rounds with unlimited 'breaks' depending on the skill of the competitors. Each round consists of three consecutive numbers: 1, 2, 3, 4, 5, 6, 7, 8, 9, 10, 11, 12, 13, 14, 15, 16, 17, 18, and 19, 20, and bulls.

The player who wins the toss scores 2 points for a double and 3 for a treble on any one of the three permitted numbers in that round: a single counts nothing but the break of the player continues. A break is over when that number is missed entirely. Apart from in round 7 (when an outer bull counts two and an inner bull three, to match the doubles and trebles of 19 and 20), either bullseye counts four away in favour of the opposing player. A round is over when both players come to the end of their breaks. The winner is the player with the higher number of points after seven rounds.

46. Share-Out One-O-One

Number of players: Two teams of two each
Number of darts: Three each

The captain of the team which wins the toss plays first, and his partner third.

The only numbers which score are 10 and 11, singles on those numbers counting 1 each, doubles two each, and trebles three each. The snag is that these scores count only if at least one dart in the set of three lands somewhere in the 10, and one other somewhere in the 11. Very good players will soon reach the magic aggregate of 101 points, the team scoring an aggregate of fifty-one first being the winner.

The less expert can go up to 51, 71, or 91 aggregate for both teams.

47. White City Dogs

Number of players: Six
Number of darts: Two each

Each player represents a greyhound at the White City dog track, and the numbers 1-6 on the scoreboard are written against the players' names.

Each player draws a number from one to six on the track, and the 'greyhound' numbered one, on the inside, tries first to score 37 with two darts. If he scores the magic 37, he is placed first, and the second 'greyhound' tries the same on track 2. Any greyhound that doesn't make 37 with two darts will try again with others that failed until the winning order is established.

In the second heat, the previous 6 becomes 1, 1 becomes 2, 2 becomes 3, 3 becomes 4, 4 becomes 5, and 5 becomes 6. This progressive numbering continues until all six players have taken each number once, over six heats. The winning 'greyhound' is the one which has collected the highest number of points over the 6 beats, scoring 6 for 1st place, 5 for 2nd, and so on.

In the pub game of White City, before a race each entrant puts 35 pence in the kitty to a total of £2.10, and at the end of each race the kitty is shared out: 60p to the winner, 50p to the 2nd, 40p to the 3rd, 30p to the 4th, 20p to the 5th and 10p to the 6th. This White City Dogs game is suitable for pay-day.

48. Triangles

Number of players: Two
Number of darts: Three each

The player who wins the toss throws his three darts within the trebles circle, forming a triangle.

Player 2 now tries to throw all his 3 darts into the triangle so formed, and obtains one point for each dart falling into the triangle, to a maximum of three.

Player 2 now throws his three darts into the circle of trebles to form a new triangle, and Player 1 tries to score three darts and three points within his opponent's triangle. The match continues until one player has scored eleven points. The art is to throw your original darts in as straight a line as possible, and as near each other as possible, to make a tiny triangle with angles as acute as you can. This game is an example of those which a skilful player can make very difficult for his rival.

49. Scram

Number of players: Two
Number of darts: Three each

The player who wins the toss is the Stopper, and his rival is the Scorer.

The Stopper throws three darts to put numbers on the board out of play: these 'stopped' numbers are chalked up on the scoreboard. The Scorer then scores as many as possible, excluding inner and outer bullseye, in the other 17 numbers, including doubles and trebles. The Stopper then throws again to take another three numbers out of play. The Scorer may only score those numbers he throws which have not previously been stopped.

At the end of the round, when all the 20 numbers have been stopped, the two players change so that the Stopper becomes the Scorer. The winner is the Scorer with the higher score at the end of the two rounds.

50. Solo Darts

Number of players: One
Number of darts: Three

Most of the games in this book can be adapted for playing on your own. In Once Round the Island, you can see how few darts you miss on the way to notching 1-20 with twenty consecutive darts. You should be able to reduce the number of misses each time. You can play solo St. Andrews by trying to reduce your aggregate score over the '18-hole course' every time you play it. Quoits can also be played solo, as can Pontoon.

Handicapping

The principles of handicapping, well established in racing and golf, can be applied to darts in several ways, to give the best players a disadvantage.

But a handicapping committee of older players must be seen to be unbiased if the method is to work properly. There must be a system of appeal against handicaps, to be judged by an umpire or arbitrator not on the committee.

One handicap is that of distance. The best players must increase the distance from which they throw in proportion to their skill.

Another is to start the less expert player at 50 or 100 to nothing if the points up are 301 or 501: again the margin between the players will depend on the difference in their abilities.

Party Games

Darts is a game for the whole family, and for every convivial occasion indoors or outdoors – wherever you can hang a board.

A game called 'Pirate's Eye-Patch' is really a party game. In the first game of two, each player has a standard eye-patch over the left eye. In the second, the standard eye-patch is placed over the right eye. The resulting disparity in scores shows yet again that darts is a more complicated game than we took it for when we started, all those years ago.

'Upsy-Daisy' is a party game for sober adults. After sufficient solo practice, you turn your back to the board, and throw the darts upward through your parted legs. The normal 501 scoring system applies, though you may take a little longer to get it, and doubles are not required to start or finish. To be played in the earlier part of the evening.

It's Your Turn!

I can hear the reader saying that his own special game of darts is better than any devised for this book. If that's true, please send a description of your game to Jabez Gotobed, c/o The Oleander Press, 16 Orchard Street, Cambridge, CB1 1JT. All the best games will be printed in the next edition of Darts, and of course the first player to submit each game published will be credited by name. Step up to the oche: it's your turn!

Printed in Great Britain
by Amazon